KT-513-440

Housework

Ruth Thomson

Watts Books
London • New York • Sydney

King's Road Primary School
Rosyth - Tel: 313470

Note for parents and teachers

The Changing Times series is soundly based on the requirements of the History Curriculum. Using the device of four generations of a real family, the author combines reminiscences of this family with other people's oral evidence. The oral history is matched with photographs and other contemporary sources. Many other lessons are hidden in the text, which practises the skills of chronological sequencing, gives reference to a timeline and introduces the language and vocabulary of the past. Young children will find much useful information here, as well as a new understanding of the recent history of everyday situations and familiar things.

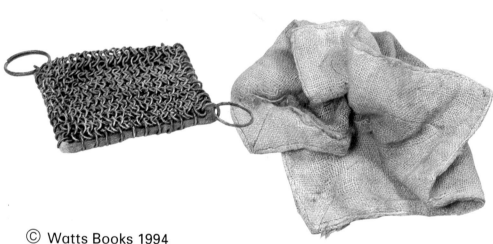

© Watts Books 1994

Paperback edition 1995

Watts Books
96 Leonard Street
London
EC2A 4RH

Franklin Watts Australia
14 Mars Road
Lane Cove
NSW 2066

UK ISBN: 0 7496 1489 7 (hardback)
UK ISBN: 0 7496 1813 2 (paperback)

Dewey Decimal Classification Number 640

A CIP catalogue record for this book is available from the British Library.

Editor: Sarah Ridley
Designer: Michael Leaman
Picture researcher: Sarah Moule

Acknowledgements: The author and publishers would like to thank the following people and organisations for their help with the preparation of this book: Archie and Alice Heasman, Bridget Virgo, Hayley and Holly and Adam Earl, Richard Wells, Helen Barden, Jenny Tong of the Cambridge and County Folk Museum, Anne Lineen of the Black Country Museum, Maureen Staniforth of Unilever, Gordon Stephenson of Reckitt and Coleman.

Printed in Malaysia

Contents

My name is Holly.
I was born in 1985.
I have got one brother
who is younger than me.

My name is Hayley.
I am Holly's mother.
I was born in 1963.

My name is Bridget.
I am Hayley's mother
and Holly's grandmother.
I was born in 1939.

My name is Alice.
I am Bridget's mother,
Hayley's grandmother
and Holly's great-grandmother.
I was born in 1914.

Mum does most of the housework in our house.

These are some of the cleaning liquids and polishes that she uses.

She cleans the stove and mops the floor.

She wipes the kitchen worktops.

Mum washes up
the dirty dishes.
Sometimes,
I help dry up.

She cleans the bath and basin
and puts bleach down the loo.

She makes the beds.

She hoovers the carpets
and dusts in all the rooms.

In winter, she lays
a fire every day
in the sitting room.

We wash our clothes
in the washing machine
and hang them up to dry.

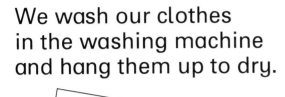

Most of our clothes
don't need ironing.
Dad irons his own shirts.

My brother and I
clean our shoes
ourselves.

I asked Mum what housework was like when she was young.

Mum said,

'My mother spent every morning cleaning.'

'At 8 o'clock, she scrubbed the doorstep and cleaned the windowsills with soapy water. People thought it was important to keep the front of their house nice.'

'Everything in sight was polished. The lino on the floors was slippery when it had just been cleaned. We fell over if we ran in too fast.'

O-Cedar

'There were squares of carpet
in the front and back rooms.
We cleaned them
with a carpet sweeper.'

'We didn't buy a hoover
until we moved to a house
with fitted carpets everywhere.'

'Our new house was
much easier
to keep clean.
We even had
a fitted kitchen.'

 **Mum now**

 **Mum aged four in 1967**

2000   1975   1950

Mum said,

'Some jobs were only done weekly, or once a month.'

'We had sheets and blankets on our beds.
The mattresses were turned and the sheets changed every week without fail.'

'We washed our sheets at home, but our neighbours sent theirs to a laundry.
A van came to collect them.'

'Some people had a window cleaner
to do their windows,
but Mum and Dad did ours.'

'One evening a week,
we lined up our shoes
and my mother gave them
all a good polish.'

I asked Mum how the washing was done.

She said,

'When I was very young,
we didn't have a washing machine.
My mother washed all our clothes
by hand in the kitchen sink.'

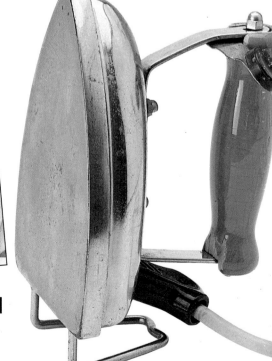

'She had an electric iron and
a wooden ironing board.'

12

'We hung the clothes out to dry.
On wet days, the clothes dried
on a wooden clothes horse
in front of the fire.'

'When we moved house,
we bought a twin tub
washing machine.
My mother felt
very up-to-date.'

I asked Granny to tell me
about housework
when she was young.

She said,

'My mother did housework
all day long, until my dad
came home for his tea.
She always wore
a pinny -
one of those
flowery ones.'

'She used brushes for everything -
hard brushes for the carpets,
soft brushes for the hearth,
a cornice brush for the ceilings,
and a scrubbing brush
for the kitchen table.'

14

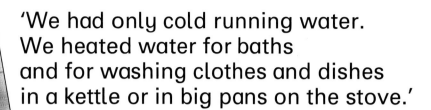

'We had only cold running water.
We heated water for baths
and for washing clothes and dishes
in a kettle or in big pans on the stove.'

'It was hard work
keeping our house clean.
My mother used to dream
of having a house
that was easier
to look after.'

2000   1975   1950

I asked my granny if she helped out.

She said,

'I used to cut newspaper into squares and string them together for the privy (an outside lavatory).'

(Newspaper) loo paper

'The privy was in a shed in the garden.
We hung the newspaper squares on a hook.'

'I also helped empty the potties in the mornings.
That wasn't a nice job.'

'Our floors were covered with lino
with squares of carpet or mats on top.'

Carpet beater

'We took the carpets outside
and beat them on the washing line
with a carpet beater.
We shook out the mats.'

I asked Granny about clothes washing.

She said,

'Washday was always
on Mondays.
It took up most of the day.
We ate cold Sunday leftovers
for dinner, because mother
never had time to cook.'

'At 7 o'clock in the morning,
Dad lit the copper
to heat the water.
He used any old rubbish as fuel.
He poured the hot water
into our big tin bath.'

'The clothes were scrubbed
with a brush and soap
against a washboard.
Then they were boiled
in clean water in the copper.
That took all morning.'

'After they were mangled, the clothes were hung outside.'

'On wet days, they were dried on a rack above the fire. I hated wet washdays. They made the house stink.'

Great-granny described what her house was like
when she was young.

She said,

'Our house had no electricity.
We had gas lighting downstairs.
It was smoky and made
everything black and sooty.'

Sacking duster

Feather duster

'The rooms had to be
dusted and swept,
and the paintwork washed
every day.'

'There was no lighting upstairs.
We took candles to bed with us.
I was petrified of the dark.'

'We didn't have a bathroom
or an inside toilet.
We washed in the bedroom
with a jug of water and a basin.'

'We took it in turns to have
a bath on a Saturday night.'

21

2000   1975   1950

Great-granny told me that housework was very hard work when she was young.

She said,

'We didn't have any machines or fancy cleaning things to help us. We used old vests for dusters and knitted our own dishcloths. We scrubbed pans with metal scourers and soda.'

Washboard for scrubbing clothes against

Block of soap

Wash tub

Pan scourer

'Clothes washing was done by hand once a week. The whites were boiled in the copper all morning and scrubbed with soap.'

Clothes pegs

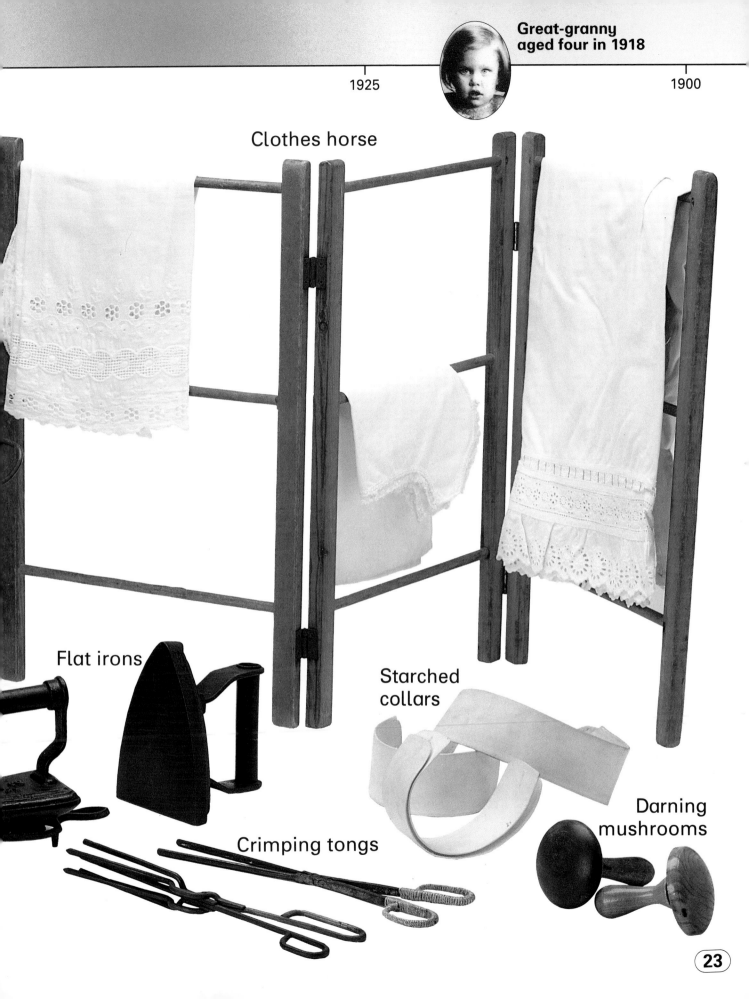

Clothes horse

Flat irons

Starched
collars

Crimping tongs

Darning
mushrooms

'We cooked on a big cast-iron stove
called a kitchener.
It kept the room nice
and warm as well.'

'We heated
hot water on it
in a big kettle.'

'Like most people, we took pride in our stove.
It took a lot of work to keep it clean.
We washed and whitened
the hearthstone until it gleamed.'

'We raked out the ashes
and black-leaded it every day.'

Bathbrick

Stove brush

'We polished
the steel bits
with bathbrick.'

'A sweep came three times a year
to clean the soot out of the chimney.
He had a big brush.
He joined on more and more sticks
to push the brush up the chimney.'

Great-granny went into service, as a live-in maid,
when she left school at thirteen.

She said,

'My parents had thirteen children.
They couldn't afford to keep me.
I went to clean for a rich old man.
His house had electricity,
posh carpets and lots of furniture.'

'I worked all day long
and every other Sunday.
The housekeeper told me
what to do.
It was hard work
and I hated it.'

'I did dirty jobs in the morning.
I cleaned the steps and the stove.'

'I made up the fires.'

'I polished the floors
until they shone.'

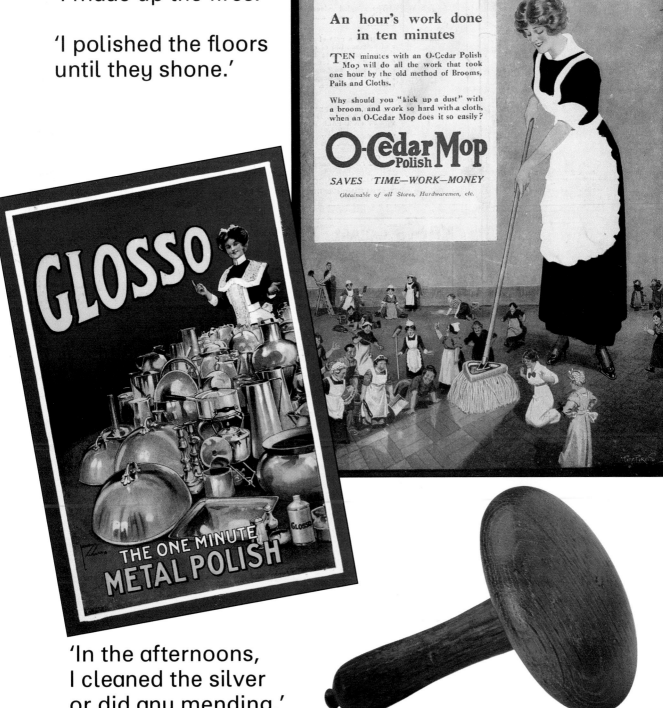

An hour's work done
in ten minutes

TEN minutes with an O-Cedar Polish
Mop will do all the work that took
one hour by the old method of Brooms,
Pails and Cloths.

Why should you "kick up a dust" with
a broom, and work so hard with a cloth,
when an O-Cedar Mop does it so easily?

O-Cedar Mop
Polish

SAVES   TIME—WORK—MONEY

Obtainable of all Stores, Hardwaremen, etc.

GLOSSO

THE ONE MINUTE
METAL POLISH

'In the afternoons,
I cleaned the silver
or did any mending.'

Darning mushroom

27

Things to do

These are some old advertisements for soaps and washing powders. Collect some modern advertisements and compare them.

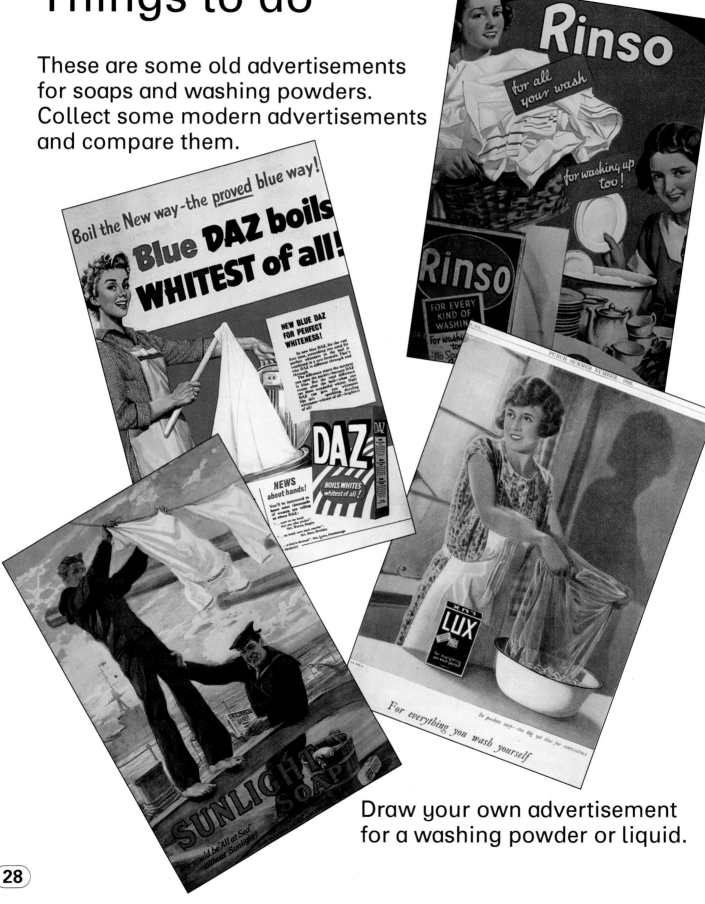

Draw your own advertisement for a washing powder or liquid.

Ask your parents and grandparents
what sort of cleaners and polishes
were used when they were young.
These pictures may help remind them.

What cleaners and polishes are used
in your house?
Are any of them still the same ?

Which things did your great-grandparents
use for cleaning?
Which did your parents and grandparents use?

Metal pan scourer

Cleaning pads

Squeezy

Brillo pads

Floor brush

Carpet sweeper

Duster

Mop and bucket

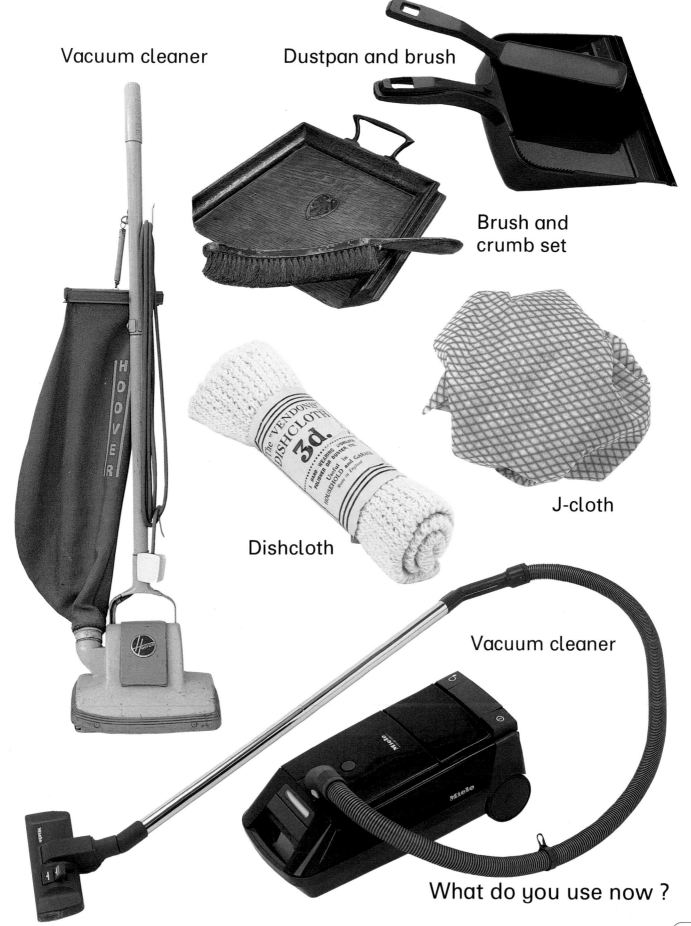

Vacuum cleaner

Dustpan and brush

Brush and crumb set

Dishcloth

J-cloth

Vacuum cleaner

What do you use now ?

31

King's Road Primary School
Rosyth - Tel: 313470

Index

Photographs: Advertising Archive 11tl, 11b;
Barnaby Picture Library 13t, 13b; Beamish
endpapers, 21cr; Martyn Chillmaid/Dudley Black
Country Museum 16tr, 17r, 18t, 18b, 20tr, 20bl,
20br, 24l, 30/31; Mary Evans Picture Library 21bl,
27tr, 27cl, 28br; Chris Fairclough cover br,
contents pg, 4-5, 6-7; Robert Harding Picture
Library 10t; Hulton Deutsch Collection Ltd cover
tr and bl, title pg(t), 8t, 12t, 12bl, 15t, 17l, 19t;
Mansell Collection 26tr; Peter Millard imprint pg,
12br, 16tl, 21tl, 22/23, 24tr, 25tl, 25tr, 27br,
29br, 30/31; Robert Opie cover tl, title pg(b),
8b, 9(all), 11c, 14c, 15b, 16b, 22bl, 26b, 28tl,
28tr, 29tr, 29b, 31tl; Picturepoint 28bl;
Popperfoto 14t, 19b, 25b; Smarts Laundry 10b;
Ruth Thomson 14bl, 29tl.